MEET THE POLICEMAN/
TE PRESENTO A LOS POLICÍAS

By Joyce Jeffries

Traducción al español: Eduardo Alamán

Gareth Stevens
Publishing

Please visit our website, www.garethstevens.com. For a free color catalog of all our high-quality books, call toll free 1-800-542-2595 or fax 1-877-542-2596.

Library of Congress Cataloging-in-Publication Data

Jeffries, Joyce.
[Meet the policeman. English & Spanish]
Meet the policeman = Te presento a los policías / Joyce Jeffries.
    p. cm. — (People around town = Gente de mi ciudad)
ISBN 978-1-4339-7390-1 (library binding)
1. Police—Juvenile literature. I. Title.
HV7922.J4418 2013
363.2—dc23

2012012857

First Edition

Published in 2013 by
Gareth Stevens Publishing
111 East 14th Street, Suite 349
New York, NY 10003

Copyright © 2013 Gareth Stevens Publishing

Editor: Katie Kawa
Designer: Andrea Davison-Bartolotta
Spanish Translation: Eduardo Alamán

Photo credits: Cover Creatas/Thinkstock; p. 1 Stockbyte/Thinkstock; p. 5 Photodisc/Thinkstock; p. 7 John Roman Images/Shutterstock.com; p. 9 Kanwarjit Singh Boparai/Shutterstock.com; pp. 11, 24 (radar gun) VladKol/Shutterstock.com; p. 13 Lisa F. Young/Shutterstock.com; p. 15 Carolina K. Smith, M. D./Shutterstock.com; p. 17 Dwight Smith/Shutterstock.com; pp. 19, 24 (uniform) Lifesize/Thinkstock; p. 21 Bill Pugliano/Stringer/Getty Images; pp. 23, 24 (mounted police) Stuart Monk/Shutterstock.com.

Printed in the United States of America

CPSIA compliance information: Batch #CS12GS: For further information contact Gareth Stevens, New York, New York at 1-800-542-2595.

Contents

Contenido

A policeman's job is
to keep people safe.

El trabajo de un policía
es proteger a las
personas.

5

He is very brave!

¡Los policías son muy valientes!

He makes sure people follow laws. These are important rules.

Los policías se aseguran de que las personas sigan las leyes. Estas leyes son importantes.

He uses a tool to see
how fast cars go.
It is a radar gun.

Los policías utilizan una
pistola especial para
ver la velocidad de los
autos. Es una pistola
radar.

He stops cars
that go too fast.

Los policías detienen
a los coches que van
demasiado rápido.

He has a special car. It has red and blue lights.

Los policías tienen un auto especial. Cuenta con luces rojas y azules.

15

The car makes
a loud noise.
This is called a siren.

Este auto hace un ruido
fuerte. Esto se llama
sirena.

Policemen wear special clothes. This is called a uniform.

Los policías se visten de forma especial. Esta ropa es un uniforme.

19

Some work with dogs.
These are K9 teams.

Algunos policías
trabajan con perros.
Estos son los equipos K9.

Mounted police ride
on horses!

- -

¡La policía montada
usa caballos!

Words to Know/
Palabras que debes saber

mounted police/
(la) policía
montada

radar gun/
(la) pistola
radar

uniform/
(el) uniforme

Index / Índice

24